THIS JOURNAL BELONGS TO

Destination Log

LOG #	DATES	DESTINATION
LOG #	DATES	DESTINATION
LOG #	DATES	DESTINATION
LOG #	DATES	DESTINATION
LOG #	DATES	DESTINATION
LOG #	DATES	DESTINATION
LOG #	DATES	DESTINATION
LOG #	DATES	DESTINATION
LOG #	DATES	DESTINATION
LOG #	DATES	DESTINATION

Travel Bucket List

PLACES TO GO

○ _____
○ _____
○ _____
○ _____
○ _____
○ _____
○ _____

ATTRACTIONS TO SEE

○ _____
○ _____
○ _____
○ _____
○ _____
○ _____
○ _____

THINGS TO DO

○ _____
○ _____
○ _____
○ _____
○ _____
○ _____
○ _____

FOODS TO TRY

○ _____
○ _____
○ _____
○ _____
○ _____
○ _____
○ _____

DARE TO DREAM

○ _____
○ _____
○ _____
○ _____
○ _____

Destination

LOG

DEPARTURE DATE _____

RETURN DATE _____

TRANSPORTATION

_____

_____

TRAVELERS

STOPS ALONG THE WAY

ACCOMMODATIONS

_____

_____

WEATHER

ACTIVITIES

○ _____

○ _____

○ _____

○ _____

○ _____

○ _____

○ _____

NEW FRIENDS

○ _____

○ _____

○ _____

○ _____

SOUVENIRS

DESTINATION RANKING

☆ ☆ ☆ ☆ ☆

RESTAURANTS & GOOD EATS

_____

_____

_____

INTERESTING SIGHTS

_____

_____

_____

FUNNY HAPPENINGS

_____

_____

_____

HIGHLIGHTS & FAVORITE MOMENTS

_____

_____

_____

EXCITING EXPERIENCES

_____

_____

_____

UNFORTUNATE MISHAPS

_____

_____

_____

Notes & Photos

Notes & Photos

Notes & Photos

Notes & Photos

Destination

LOG

DEPARTURE DATE _____

RETURN DATE _____

TRANSPORTATION

_____

_____

STOPS ALONG THE WAY

TRAVELERS

ACCOMMODATIONS

_____

_____

ACTIVITIES

○ _____

○ _____

○ _____

○ _____

○ _____

○ _____

○ _____

WEATHER

NEW FRIENDS

○ _____

○ _____

○ _____

○ _____

SOUVENIRS

DESTINATION RANKING

☆ ☆ ☆ ☆ ☆

RESTAURANTS & GOOD EATS

_____

_____

_____

_____

INTERESTING SIGHTS

_____

_____

_____

_____

FUNNY HAPPENINGS

_____

_____

_____

_____

HIGHLIGHTS & FAVORITE MOMENTS

_____

_____

_____

_____

EXCITING EXPERIENCES

_____

_____

_____

_____

UNFORTUNATE MISHAPS

_____

_____

_____

_____

Notes & Photos

Notes & Photos

Notes & Photos

Notes & Photos

Destination

LOG

DEPARTURE DATE _____

RETURN DATE _____

TRANSPORTATION

_____

_____

TRAVELERS

STOPS ALONG THE WAY

ACCOMMODATIONS

_____

_____

ACTIVITIES

○ _____

○ _____

○ _____

○ _____

○ _____

○ _____

○ _____

WEATHER

NEW FRIENDS

○ _____

○ _____

○ _____

○ _____

SOUVENIRS

DESTINATION RANKING

☆ ☆ ☆ ☆ ☆

RESTAURANTS & GOOD EATS

_____

_____

_____

_____

INTERESTING SIGHTS

_____

_____

_____

_____

FUNNY HAPPENINGS

_____

_____

_____

_____

HIGHLIGHTS & FAVORITE MOMENTS

_____

_____

_____

_____

EXCITING EXPERIENCES

_____

_____

_____

_____

UNFORTUNATE MISHAPS

_____

_____

_____

_____

Notes & Photos

Notes & Photos

Notes & Photos

Notes & Photos

Destination

DEPARTURE DATE

RETURN DATE

TRANSPORTATION

STOPS ALONG THE WAY

TRAVELERS

ACCOMMODATIONS

ACTIVITIES
- ○
- ○
- ○
- ○
- ○
- ○
- ○

WEATHER

NEW FRIENDS
- ○
- ○
- ○
- ○

SOUVENIRS

DESTINATION RANKING

☆ ☆ ☆ ☆ ☆

RESTAURANTS & GOOD EATS

INTERESTING SIGHTS

FUNNY HAPPENINGS

HIGHLIGHTS & FAVORITE MOMENTS

EXCITING EXPERIENCES

UNFORTUNATE MISHAPS

Notes & Photos

Notes & Photos

Notes & Photos

Notes & Photos

Destination

LOG

DEPARTURE DATE _____

RETURN DATE _____

TRANSPORTATION

_____

_____

TRAVELERS

ACTIVITIES

○ _____

○ _____

○ _____

○ _____

○ _____

○ _____

○ _____

SOUVENIRS

STOPS ALONG THE WAY

ACCOMMODATIONS

_____

_____

WEATHER

NEW FRIENDS

○ _____

○ _____

○ _____

○ _____

DESTINATION RANKING

☆ ☆ ☆ ☆ ☆

RESTAURANTS & GOOD EATS

_____

_____

_____

_____

INTERESTING SIGHTS

_____

_____

_____

_____

FUNNY HAPPENINGS

_____

_____

_____

_____

HIGHLIGHTS & FAVORITE MOMENTS

_____

_____

_____

_____

EXCITING EXPERIENCES

_____

_____

_____

_____

UNFORTUNATE MISHAPS

_____

_____

_____

_____

Notes & Photos

Notes & Photos

Notes & Photos

Notes & Photos

Destination

DEPARTURE DATE

RETURN DATE

TRANSPORTATION

TRAVELERS

ACTIVITIES
- ◯
- ◯
- ◯
- ◯
- ◯
- ◯
- ◯

SOUVENIRS

STOPS ALONG THE WAY

ACCOMMODATIONS

WEATHER

NEW FRIENDS
- ◯
- ◯
- ◯
- ◯

DESTINATION RANKING

☆ ☆ ☆ ☆ ☆

RESTAURANTS & GOOD EATS

_____

_____

_____

_____

INTERESTING SIGHTS

_____

_____

_____

_____

FUNNY HAPPENINGS

_____

_____

_____

_____

HIGHLIGHTS & FAVORITE MOMENTS

_____

_____

_____

_____

EXCITING EXPERIENCES

_____

_____

_____

_____

UNFORTUNATE MISHAPS

_____

_____

_____

_____

Notes & Photos

Notes & Photos

Notes & Photos

Notes & Photos

Destination

LOG

DEPARTURE DATE _____

RETURN DATE _____

TRANSPORTATION
_____
_____

STOPS ALONG THE WAY

TRAVELERS

ACCOMMODATIONS
_____
_____

ACTIVITIES

○ _____
○ _____
○ _____
○ _____
○ _____
○ _____
○ _____

WEATHER

NEW FRIENDS

○ _____
○ _____
○ _____
○ _____

SOUVENIRS

DESTINATION RANKING

☆ ☆ ☆ ☆ ☆

RESTAURANTS & GOOD EATS

_____

_____

_____

_____

INTERESTING SIGHTS

_____

_____

_____

_____

FUNNY HAPPENINGS

_____

_____

_____

_____

HIGHLIGHTS & FAVORITE MOMENTS

_____

_____

_____

_____

EXCITING EXPERIENCES

_____

_____

_____

_____

UNFORTUNATE MISHAPS

_____

_____

_____

Notes & Photos

Notes & Photos

Notes & Photos

Notes & Photos

Destination

LOG

DEPARTURE DATE
_____

RETURN DATE
_____

TRANSPORTATION
_____
_____

TRAVELERS

STOPS ALONG THE WAY

ACCOMMODATIONS
_____
_____

ACTIVITIES
- ○ _____
- ○ _____
- ○ _____
- ○ _____
- ○ _____
- ○ _____
- ○ _____

WEATHER

NEW FRIENDS
- ○ _____
- ○ _____
- ○ _____
- ○ _____

SOUVENIRS

DESTINATION RANKING

☆ ☆ ☆ ☆ ☆

RESTAURANTS & GOOD EATS

_____

_____

_____

_____

INTERESTING SIGHTS

_____

_____

_____

_____

FUNNY HAPPENINGS

_____

_____

_____

_____

HIGHLIGHTS & FAVORITE MOMENTS

_____

_____

_____

_____

EXCITING EXPERIENCES

_____

_____

_____

_____

UNFORTUNATE MISHAPS

_____

_____

_____

_____

Notes & Photos

Notes & Photos

Notes & Photos

Notes & Photos

Destination

LOG

DEPARTURE DATE _____

RETURN DATE _____

TRANSPORTATION

_____

_____

STOPS ALONG THE WAY

TRAVELERS

ACCOMMODATIONS

_____

_____

ACTIVITIES

- ○ _____
- ○ _____
- ○ _____
- ○ _____
- ○ _____
- ○ _____
- ○ _____

WEATHER

NEW FRIENDS

- ○ _____
- ○ _____
- ○ _____
- ○ _____

SOUVENIRS

DESTINATION RANKING

☆ ☆ ☆ ☆ ☆

RESTAURANTS & GOOD EATS

_____
_____
_____
_____

INTERESTING SIGHTS

_____
_____
_____
_____

FUNNY HAPPENINGS

_____
_____
_____
_____

HIGHLIGHTS & FAVORITE MOMENTS

_____
_____
_____
_____

EXCITING EXPERIENCES

_____
_____
_____
_____

UNFORTUNATE MISHAPS

_____
_____
_____
_____

Notes & Photos

Notes & Photos

Notes & Photos

Notes & Photos

Destination

LOG

DEPARTURE DATE

RETURN DATE

TRANSPORTATION

STOPS ALONG THE WAY

TRAVELERS

ACCOMMODATIONS

ACTIVITIES

- ○
- ○
- ○
- ○
- ○
- ○
- ○

WEATHER

NEW FRIENDS

- ○
- ○
- ○
- ○

SOUVENIRS

DESTINATION RANKING

☆ ☆ ☆ ☆ ☆

RESTAURANTS & GOOD EATS

_____

_____

_____

_____

INTERESTING SIGHTS

_____

_____

_____

_____

FUNNY HAPPENINGS

_____

_____

_____

_____

HIGHLIGHTS & FAVORITE MOMENTS

_____

_____

_____

_____

EXCITING EXPERIENCES

_____

_____

_____

_____

UNFORTUNATE MISHAPS

_____

_____

_____

_____

Notes & Photos

Notes & Photos

Notes & Photos

Notes & Photos

Thank you for your purchase!

We hope you've enjoyed your Travel Diary!

As a small business, we very much appreciate your feedback. Please scan the QR code below to leave a review or re-order on Amazon.

This journal is printed and sold by Amazon. If there is an issue with the print quality of this journal, please contact Amazon Customer Service.

Thank you for your business!

DESIGNS

Made in United States
North Haven, CT
09 September 2022

23929557R00043